This journal belongs to :

_____

My 90-Day Journey Begins on:

Date: _____

My 90-Day Journey Ended on:

Date: _____

A 90-Day Journey to Mindfulness

A.S.E. Tools For Intuitives

BY LULU EYE LOVE

Dedicated to my Grandson, Button.

A Word

By Lulu Eye Love

As an Intuitive, the inner standing required to grow daily-spiritually takes time to somewhat master. We are always learning as we live; remembering is vital here.

The journey that has led up to this planner has been what seems like a lifetime. I have learned through pain, love, patience, persistence, awareness, NDE, and stillness.

Mindfulness became essential in developing, honing, and sharing my gifts from a relative state, whether from this lifetime or another. Cultivating mindfulness creates the ability to live moment-to-moment and place judgment aside.

Being in the moment is essential when considering becoming more open and allowing. I pray this book helps you reach the point of becoming more mindful, present, and aware. If not, please pass it to someone; it may help.

Introduction

House of Oshun is a spiritual home for the intuitive community. Our doors are open to emerging, senior, and entrepreneurial intuitives from all walks of life. It is our mission to encourage ascension and spiritual expansion (A.S.E.), which are never-ending processes. With great confidence, integrity, and love, we embrace our responsibility to provide the tools necessary for spiritual growth.

The House of Oshun's "A.S.E. Tools for Intuitives" is a series of books, journals, and manuals, which are designed to promote and encourage A.S.E. on many levels. The tools are created by Lulu Eye Love, a Practitioner of Intuitive Coaching and Consulting.

Each of us embody life in a physical body in which we learn from situations, life events, and individuals. How we deal with our environments at any given time determines if we are mindful and aware enough to graduate or ascend by doing the work needed to reach the next level in life.

Introduction

This journal is created and provided as a conscious guidepost to becoming more mindful, present, and aware. I believe anything one can do for 24 hours; one can do it for one week. Furthermore, anything one can do for one week; you can do it for one month. Moreover, that is how a habit forms.

The act of mindfulness is the equivalent to being in a constant meditation-like state (for lack of better wording, dah'ling). Here, you need to keep track of your observations daily for 90 days. If a day is missed, merely begin in your current space. There is no catching up, only catching IN-the-now! Enjoy life moment by moment and step by step!

When utilizing mindfulness, you train yourself to be attentive, present, and kind. This training entails a focus on self-love and happiness. To become one with the world, you must first become one with yourself and your immediate environment (your world).

Understanding the effectiveness of being present helps clear the mind to welcome intuitive guidance, directly or indirectly, via divine assistance. By learning to heal and correct yourself on YOUR life path as an Intuitive, you will become well-suited to assist others more effectively!

A.S.E!

1) ASCENSION

The goal of having a hue-man experience as a spiritual being is illumination or ascension, and it may take many incarnations to reach our ascended goals. Our souls often want us to go back to Earth, meet the same people, and experience similar situations to re-live the challenge or complete unresolved karmic contracts.

2) MINDFULNESS

- Living in the now (i.e., the present moment)
- Seeing things for what they are and how they play a part inside and outside your life
- Relating to life from a space of compassion
- The art of understanding on a soul level
- The ability to notice and comprehend certain synchronicities
- The roadmap to freedom
- The observation of thoughts and feelings, people and places, things and situations
- The release of judgment and the pure knowing that all things have a time and space
- To be in tune with your Higher Self & the collective consciousness

A.S.E!

3) WHO WILL BENEFIT FROM THIS JOURNAL

- **The Entrepreneurial Intuitive**^{SM}- Professional Intuitives currently using their gifts on the spiritual market. They are interested in using A.S.E. TOOLS for Intuitives as a guide to help grow their business and mentor Emerging Intuitives.

- **The Emerging Intuitive**^{SM}- Intuitives who are developing and honing their skills. They are delving deeper into their practice, becoming more in tune with their Higher Self, and strengthening their connection to Spirit. Emerging Intuitives are learning how to trust, embrace, and have more confidence in their natural gifts and talents.

- **The Senior Intuitive**^{SM}- Intuitives who have a spiritual practice, or are reconnecting to it. They are interested in becoming an Entrepreneurial Intuitive and have a strong desire to recreate and build their practice.

A.S.E!

4 TRAITS OF OUR IDEAL A.S.E. CLIENTS

1. **Mindful-** We work with clients who are seeking spiritual, personal, and financial growth. Our courses are designed to guide you through the process of understanding why you keep experiencing unfavorable results. By practicing mindfulness, you will learn how to utilize our systems, practices, and spiritual success principles to continuously grow and transform.

2. **Present-** You value mentorship. You appreciate the support and coaching you receive. You are ready to work with a coach, who will show you the path to creating the life you want. Our tools have been designed to help you practice the art of being present in every situation. You accept responsibility for the results you see or don't see based on your actions, or inactions.

A.S.E!

4 TRAITS OF OUR IDEAL A.S.E. CLIENTS

3. Aware- You are confident that we can provide you with the tools necessary to change, and transform your life. You are ready to let go of patterns and behaviors that no longer serve you. Our courses have been designed to push, and guide you towards seeking the most favorable outcome in a situation.

4. Present- You value mentor-ship. You appreciate the support and coaching you receive. You are ready to work with a coach, who will show you the path to creating the life you want. Our tools have been designed to help you practice the art of being present in every situation. You accept responsibility for the results you see or don't see based on your actions, or inaction's.

5. Self-Accountability- You accept responsibility for your growth and transformation. You are willing to listen, learn, take action, and follow through with the individualized curriculum that has been created for you.

A.S.E!

Our clients hold themselves accountable for putting their best effort towards the great change and transformation they desire in their lives.

This journal was created to help it's owner to become more aware and present. Being mindful on a moment-by-moment basis would be nearly impossible to record. Speaking of 'record,' try recording your observations and synchronicities as you may throughout the day to keep track of daily milestones. It would be a good idea to carry a small notepad on your person.

The very first thing you will need to do is CLEAR THE CLUTTER. Clearing the clutter will help interpret your thoughts, feelings, reactions/inaction's, synchronicities, and motives. Thus, you will gain insights and clarity regarding how you deal with daily challenges and what changes may be necessary for you to incorporate into your life to become more mindful, present, and aware of your behavior patterns.

It is critical to sort through daily activities and events as often as possible until the process becomes a way of life. This will help you realize what you can/cannot control. What is or is not deserving of your attention at any given time.

Clear The Clutter: Vent

When you put in the effort to relearn your true nature and align with your true north, there are many benefits to clearing the clutter via venting.

You see, the brain is not wired to split attention in too many different directions. It is good to be organized, at peace, and aware for one to fully filter information into the right mental files and have a clear perception of what is of the utmost priority on your journey at any given time.

To have your brain at this ideal state, you will need to make space by clearing some mental clutter.

Decluttering your mind will help you become more aware of things that are worth your time, effort, feelings, and attention. As you move along your mindful journey, you will notice how the clutter will decrease and your observations will increase.

Advantages of decluttering: It creates peace of mind, and provides more time and attention for those things in your life you deem valuable or worthy of your focus. Thus, leaving more time, appreciation, and space for the people and activities you choose enables you to be more present and mindful.

Clear The Clutter: Sacred Space

When it comes to becoming more mindful, it is vital to spend time in sacred space. Sacred space allows you just to be one with the ONE, not having to think, sort things out, or analyze, but to be open, rest, and allow your truths to be revealed.

Go into your sacred space with your journal. A ten-minute meditation should suffice. By meditating at this time, you will want to detach from the ego. When you are prepared to move forward (you will know), begin to clear the clutter at this time.

Allow the information to flow without forcing your thoughts. Complete sentences are not crucial in automatic writing because it will all make sense to you. No one else is reading it. Allowing your higher self to guide you at this point will be very beneficial. You can ask (after or during meditation) that only beings of the highest light, unconditional love, and compassion, provide what is needed to know on this day. Begin.

Clear The Clutter : Automatic Writing

This practice will take some getting used to, but it is very doable. The best reason for practicing mindful observations (as prescribed by this journal) is that it brings you into the present moment with a bit of past influence (i.e., your day). It's especially useful if you're having trouble getting your mind to focus, mastering your emotions, realigning with your true north, or getting your mind off the future.

Automatic writing is sourced from the unconscious mind, a doorway into the soul realm, or your Star-Player connection. Automatic writing is an excellent way to gain guidance! All you will need to learn is how to empty the mind when entering your sacred space.

Here is another example of recognizing the treasure in your clutter... To begin, highlight three things in your clutter that stand out the most. For each highlight, notice your feelings, thoughts, and what actions you may have taken and why. Here is where your automatic writing/answers come into play. It is time to allow observations on a soul level to subsequently unveiled to your conscious mind.

Clear The Clutter: Sample Questions

1. What was the focal point of the day? (i.e., faith, arrogance, individuality, patience, dedication, health, fitness, jealousy, kindness, boundaries, fairness, or confidence, et cetera.) You may have more than one focal point but notice the more dominant theme.

2. Were there any synchronicities that led up to the focal point of the day? Perhaps numbers, conversations, songs, events, or inner voices rattling about at certain times?

3. How did you feel, or what were your thoughts as you observed the synchronicities? Why did you feel or think in that way? Did you follow your inner voice, or did you make a decision based on your thoughts?

4. Did you notice your mood change or any feelings associated with certain things you wrote? Why is this?

The Logging Page

1. **Date** - assists with the growth overview; you will have the ability to review your growth in 30-day increments as a result. Weigh what still requires work or adjustments, and where you have genuinely graduated.

2. Mood - helps re-evaluate what may or may not have triggered you and if/why you were triggered and by whom/what. You can record this daily until it becomes completely natural. Self-observation from an ethical standpoint is how we graduate. Also, your mood may trigger your affirmation for the day. (i.e., sad? Affirm: I AM filled with joy, understanding, and positive vibes!)

3. Meditation - at least twice daily assists you with aligning with your higher self (true north) until you begin to do this unconsciously—although we all fall off every so often...that's life! Working on your meditative breathing throughout the day should become a subconscious effort by the end of your 90-day journey.

4. Recenter/Refocus - how often it takes and how you do so is very important for re-evaluation at the end of the 90 days. It will show how far you have come, and how much you have grown in such a short time frame. By the 30th day you should be in a space where it is a natural shift.

The Logging Page

5. Clarity is where you are very honest with yourself about your mental state, feelings, spirit, body, and synchronicities (i.e., what you learn about yourself and others on a daily basis). It gives you the keys to becoming more successful at being mindful and correcting your thinking, feelings, and overall spiritual health.

It is essential to keep in mind that we are all a tiny part of a whole. We play our role and work from a space of unconditional love and light, and also welcome the dark (i.e., shadow aspects) for continued growth. Shadow work can be daunting at times; however, it is included and is a growth requirement. Make peace with that as you move along your life-path.

Things that may interrupt mindfulness...

- Poor listening and lack luster communication skills when in conversation with others: it is important to actively listen and respond from a mindful space. Communicating with the intent to hear the other person without pre-conceived notions or feeling the need to assume you know what they are conveying without allowing the other to completely express themselves.
- Racing or an influx of thoughts which can be triggered by any number of things. You may become so involved with thinking, that you over-think or over-analyze to the point that you are no longer living in the present moment.
- Cell phones, social media, television, entertaining NOUNS whom take you out of your element or do not serve your highest good, et cetera.
- Worry, stress, anxiety, forgetting to focus on your breath when feeling overwhelmed throughout the day.
- Asking yourself the questions needed to recenter
- Not aligning with your true north in the a.m. and throughout the day.
- Allowing things out of your control to consume you to the point of re-pressing which leads to de-pression or a tower moment! (shadow work)
- Diet!

Affirmations

Affirmations are an excellent way to keep mental balance, create life experiences, among many other benefits. Whenever a negative thought or uneasy feeling comes to the forefront, affirmations are an excellent way to change and re-direct your mood. By choosing at least one positive affirmation as your primary focus for the day, will allow you to have a go-to for re-calibrating and immediate realigning when needed.

Speak life into your being! The use of affirmations can be a powerful tool when used appropriately. There are also affirmations available online in which you can listen to during your slumber or as a part of your morning routine. So it is!

Notes

There are 30 pages in the back of the journal, which are available for jotting extra notes. I would suggest you jot research notes and random thoughts that derive from your daily journaling.

Now Let's Get Started!

A.S.E. Worksheet

This worksheet begins your 90-Day Journey to Mindfulness. Please take your time to answer the questions below. Doing so will help you ground your expectations in a way that will provide that you may review your progress and achieve your goals. You can consider this as your first mindfulness practice: by being mindful of your intentions and commitment to the beginning process.

So, first, something drew you to this journey, which made it seem like an opportunity to grow.

For instance, you may have noticed different synchronicity types or want to learn to quiet your mind better. You may find yourself having trouble concentrating, feel a need to connect to your Star Player more effectively, or maybe you have been suffering from low self-worth, et cetera.

You may be very sensitive and want to have more control over your energy and interactions with others. Or you may want to increase your ability to be present and fully engaged in life, to accept more fully yourself, others, just as you and they are.

A.S.E. WORKSHEET

Name _____   Date _____

UPON COMPLETION OF THIS 90-DAY JOURNEY I EXPECT THAT:

WHEN AND WHERE WILL YOU LOG IN YOUR JOURNAL DAILY?

A.S.E. WORKSHEET

10 POSITIVE THINGS ABOUT YOU:

A.S.E. WORKSHEET

10 THINGS YOU ARE GRATEFUL FOR:

A.S.E. WORKSHEET

10 THINGS YOU WANT TO CHANGE ABOUT YOURSELF:

Time to do the work!

Clear the Clutter

DATE: _____

A 90-DAY JOURNEY TO MINDFULNESS

DATE: _____

AM MOOD ☺ ☹ 😫

PM MOOD ☺ ☹ 😫

Meditation:

AM Minutes _____

PM Minutes _____

Today's Affirmation:

AM Grattitude:

PM Gratttude:

Mindful Observations Today:

Mood Change: _____

Conscious Recenter/Refocus : _____

Subconscious Re-center/Refocus : _____

Clarity :

Clear the Clutter

DATE: _____

A 90-DAY JOURNEY TO MINDFULNESS

DATE: _____

AM MOOD ☺ ☹ 😫

PM MOOD ☺ ☹ 😫

Meditation:

AM Minutes _____

PM Minutes _____

Today's Affirmation:

AM Grattitude:

PM Gratttude:

Mindful Observations Today:

Mood Change: _____

Conscious Recenter/Refocus : _____

Subconscious Re-center/Refocus : _____

Clarity :

Clear the Clutter

DATE: _____

A 90-DAY JOURNEY TO MINDFULNESS

Meditation:

AM Minutes _____

PM Minutes _____

Today's Affirmation:

AM Grattitude:

PM Gratttude:

Mindful Observations Today:

Mood Change: _____

Conscious Recenter/Refocus : _____

Subconscious Re-center/Refocus : _____

Clarity :

Clear the Clutter

DATE: _____

DATE: _____

AM MOOD

PM MOOD

Meditation:

AM Minutes _____

PM Minutes _____

Today's Affirmation:

AM Grattitude:

PM Gratttude:

Mindful Observations Today:

Mood Change: _____

Conscious Recenter/Refocus : _____

Subconscious Re-center/Refocus : _____

Clarity :

Clear the Clutter

DATE: _____

A 90-DAY JOURNEY TO MINDFULNESS

DATE: _____

AM MOOD ☺ ☹ 😫

PM MOOD ☺ ☹ 😫

Meditation:

AM Minutes _____

PM Minutes _____

Today's Affirmation:

AM Grattitude:

PM Gratttude:

Mindful Observations Today:

Mood Change: _____

Conscious Recenter/Refocus : _____

Subconscious Re-center/Refocus : _____

Clarity :

Clear the Clutter

DATE: _____

A 90-DAY JOURNEY TO MINDFULNESS

DATE: _____

AM MOOD ☺ ☹ 😩

PM MOOD ☺ ☹ 😩

Meditation:

AM Minutes _____

PM Minutes _____

Today's Affirmation:

AM Grattitude:

PM Gratttude:

Mindful Observations Today:

Mood Change: _____

Conscious Recenter/Refocus : _____

Subconscious Re-center/Refocus :
_____

Clarity :

Clear the Clutter

DATE: _____

A 90-DAY JOURNEY TO MINDFULNESS

Meditation:

AM Minutes _____

PM Minutes _____

Today's Affirmation:

AM Grattitude:

PM Gratttude:

Mindful Observations Today:

Mood Change: _____

Conscious Recenter/Refocus : _____

Subconscious Re-center/Refocus : _____

Clarity :

Clear the Clutter

DATE: _____

A 90-DAY JOURNEY TO
MINDFULNESS

DATE: _____

AM MOOD ☺ ☹ 😖

PM MOOD ☺ ☹ 😖

Meditation:

AM Minutes _____

PM Minutes _____

Today's Affirmation:

AM Grattitude:

PM Gratttude:

Mindful Observations Today:

Mood Change: _____

Conscious Recenter/Refocus : _____

Subconscious Re-center/Refocus : _____

Clarity :

Clear the Clutter

DATE: _____

A 90-DAY JOURNEY TO MINDFULNESS

DATE: _____

AM MOOD

PM MOOD

Meditation:

AM Minutes _____

PM Minutes _____

Today's Affirmation:

AM Grattitude:

PM Gratttude:

Mindful Observations Today:

Mood Change: _____

Conscious Recenter/Refocus : _____

Subconscious Re-center/Refocus : _____

Clarity :

Clear the Clutter

DATE: _____

A 90-DAY JOURNEY TO MINDFULNESS

DATE: _____

AM MOOD ☺ ☹ 😫

PM MOOD ☺ ☹ 😫

Meditation:

AM Minutes _____

PM Minutes _____

Today's Affirmation:

AM Grattitude:

PM Gratttude:

Mindful Observations Today:

Mood Change: _____

Conscious Recenter/Refocus : _____

Subconscious Re-center/Refocus : _____

Clarity :

Clear the Clutter

DATE: _____

A 90-DAY JOURNEY TO MINDFULNESS

DATE: _____

AM MOOD ☺ ☹ 😫

PM MOOD ☺ ☹ 😫

Meditation:

AM Minutes _____

PM Minutes _____

Today's Affirmation:

AM Grattitude:

PM Gratttude:

Mindful Observations Today:

Mood Change: _____

Conscious Recenter/Refocus : _____

Subconscious Re-center/Refocus : _____

Clarity :

Clear the Clutter

DATE: _____

DATE: _____

AM MOOD ☺ ☹ 😖

PM MOOD ☺ ☹ 😖

Meditation:

AM Minutes _____

PM Minutes _____

Today's Affirmation:

AM Grattitude:

PM Gratttude:

Mindful Observations Today:

Mood Change: _____

Conscious Recenter/Refocus : _____

Subconscious Re-center/Refocus : _____

Clarity :

Clear the Clutter

DATE: _____

A 90-DAY JOURNEY TO MINDFULNESS

DATE: _____

AM MOOD

PM MOOD

Meditation:

AM Minutes _____

PM Minutes _____

Today's Affirmation:

AM Grattitude:

PM Gratttude:

Mindful Observations Today:

Mood Change: _____

Conscious Recenter/Refocus : _____

Subconscious Re-center/Refocus : _____

Clarity :

Clear the Clutter

DATE: _____

A 90-DAY JOURNEY TO MINDFULNESS

DATE: _____

AM MOOD ☺ ☹ 😫

PM MOOD ☺ ☹ 😫

Meditation:

AM Minutes _____

PM Minutes _____

Today's Affirmation:

AM Grattitude:

PM Gratttude:

Mindful Observations Today:

Mood Change: _____

Conscious Recenter/Refocus : _____

Subconscious Re-center/Refocus :

Clarity :

Clear the Clutter

DATE: _____

DATE: _____

AM MOOD

PM MOOD

Meditation:

AM Minutes _____

PM Minutes _____

Today's Affirmation:

AM Grattitude:

PM Gratttude:

Mindful Observations Today:

Mood Change: _____

Conscious Recenter/Refocus : _____

Subconscious Re-center/Refocus : _____

Clarity :

Clear the Clutter

DATE: _____

DATE: _____

AM MOOD

PM MOOD

Meditation:

AM Minutes _____

PM Minutes _____

Today's Affirmation:

AM Grattitude:

PM Gratttude:

Mindful Observations Today:

Mood Change: _____

Conscious Recenter/Refocus : _____

Subconscious Re-center/Refocus : _____

Clarity :

Clear the Clutter

DATE: _____

DATE: _____

AM MOOD ☺ ☹ 😩

PM MOOD ☺ ☹ 😩

Meditation:

AM Minutes _____

PM Minutes _____

Today's Affirmation:

AM Grattitude:

PM Gratttude:

Mindful Observations Today:

Mood Change: _____

Conscious Recenter/Refocus : _____

Subconscious Re-center/Refocus : _____

Clarity :

Clear the Clutter

DATE: _____

DATE: _____

AM MOOD

PM MOOD ☺ ☹ 😩

Meditation:

AM Minutes _____

PM Minutes _____

Today's Affirmation:

AM Grattitude:

PM Gratttude:

Mindful Observations Today:

Mood Change: _____

Conscious Recenter/Refocus : _____

Subconscious Re-center/Refocus : _____

Clarity :

Clear the Clutter

DATE: _____

DATE: _____

AM MOOD ☺ ☹ 😫

PM MOOD ☺ ☹ 😫

Meditation:

AM Minutes _____

PM Minutes _____

Today's Affirmation:

AM Grattitude:

PM Gratttude:

Mindful Observations Today:

Mood Change: _____

Conscious Recenter/Refocus : _____

Subconscious Re-center/Refocus : _____

Clarity :

Clear the Clutter

DATE: _____

A 90-DAY JOURNEY TO MINDFULNESS

DATE: _____

AM MOOD ☺ ☹ 😫

PM MOOD ☺ ☹ 😫

Meditation:

AM Minutes _____

PM Minutes _____

Today's Affirmation:

AM Grattitude:

PM Gratttude:

Mindful Observations Today:

Mood Change: _____

Conscious Recenter/Refocus : _____

Subconscious Re-center/Refocus : _____

Clarity :

Clear the Clutter

DATE: _____

A 90-DAY JOURNEY TO MINDFULNESS

DATE: _____

AM MOOD

PM MOOD ☺ ☹ 😫

Meditation:

AM Minutes _____

PM Minutes _____

Today's Affirmation:

AM Grattitude:

PM Gratttude:

Mindful Observations Today:

Mood Change: _____

Conscious Recenter/Refocus : _____

Subconscious Re-center/Refocus :

_____

Clarity :

Clear the Clutter

DATE: _____

A 90-DAY JOURNEY TO MINDFULNESS

DATE: _____

AM MOOD ☺ ☹ 😫

PM MOOD ☺ ☹ 😫

Meditation:

AM Minutes _____

PM Minutes _____

Today's Affirmation:

AM Grattitude:

PM Gratttude:

Mindful Observations Today:

Mood Change: _____

Conscious Recenter/Refocus : _____

Subconscious Re-center/Refocus : _____

Clarity :

Clear the Clutter

DATE: _____

A 90-DAY JOURNEY TO MINDFULNESS

AM MOOD ☺ ☹ 😩

PM MOOD ☺ ☹ 😩

Meditation:

AM Minutes _____

PM Minutes _____

Today's Affirmation:

AM Grattitude:

PM Gratttude:

Mindful Observations Today:

Mood Change: _____

Conscious Recenter/Refocus : _____

Subconscious Re-center/Refocus :

Clarity :

Clear the Clutter

DATE: _____

DATE: _____

AM MOOD

PM MOOD

Meditation:

AM Minutes _____

PM Minutes _____

Today's Affirmation:

AM Grattitude:

PM Gratttude:

Mindful Observations Today:

Mood Change: _____

Conscious Recenter/Refocus : _____

Subconscious Re-center/Refocus : _____

Clarity :

Clear the Clutter

DATE: _____

A 90-DAY JOURNEY TO MINDFULNESS

DATE: _____

AM MOOD ☺ ☹ 😫
PM MOOD ☺ ☹ 😫

Meditation:

AM Minutes _____

PM Minutes _____

Today's Affirmation:

AM Grattitude:

PM Gratttude:

Mindful Observations Today:

Mood Change: _____

Conscious Recenter/Refocus : _____

Subconscious Re-center/Refocus : _____

Clarity :

Clear the Clutter

DATE: _____

DATE: _____

AM MOOD

PM MOOD ☺ ☹ 😫

Meditation:

AM Minutes _____

PM Minutes _____

Today's Affirmation:

AM Grattitude:

PM Gratttude:

Mindful Observations Today:

Mood Change: _____

Conscious Recenter/Refocus : _____

Subconscious Re-center/Refocus : _____

Clarity :

Clear the Clutter

DATE: _____

A 90-DAY JOURNEY TO MINDFULNESS

Meditation:

AM Minutes _____

PM Minutes _____

Today's Affirmation:

AM Grattitude:

PM Gratttude:

Mindful Observations Today:

Mood Change: _____

Conscious Recenter/Refocus : _____

Subconscious Re-center/Refocus : _____

Clarity :

Clear the Clutter

DATE: _____

A 90-DAY JOURNEY TO MINDFULNESS

DATE: _____

AM MOOD ☺ ☹ 😫

PM MOOD ☺ ☹ 😫

Meditation:

AM Minutes _____

PM Minutes _____

Today's Affirmation:

AM Grattitude:

PM Gratttude:

Mindful Observations Today:

Mood Change: _____

Conscious Recenter/Refocus : _____

Subconscious Re-center/Refocus : _____

Clarity :

Clear the Clutter

DATE: _____

A 90-DAY JOURNEY TO MINDFULNESS

DATE: _____

AM MOOD ☺ ☹ 😩

PM MOOD ☺ ☹ 😩

Meditation:

AM Minutes _____

PM Minutes _____

Today's Affirmation:

AM Grattitude:

PM Gratttude:

Mindful Observations Today:

Mood Change: _____

Conscious Recenter/Refocus : _____

Subconscious Re-center/Refocus : _____

Clarity :

Clear the Clutter

DATE: _____

A 90-DAY JOURNEY TO MINDFULNESS

DATE: _____

AM MOOD ☺ ☹ 😫

PM MOOD ☺ ☹ 😫

Meditation:

AM Minutes _____

PM Minutes _____

Today's Affirmation:

AM Grattitude:

PM Gratttude:

Mindful Observations Today:

Mood Change: _____

Conscious Recenter/Refocus : _____

Subconscious Re-center/Refocus : _____

Clarity :

30 Day Review

Let's Review your growth!

Now you have reached your first milestone. Woohoo! This review should be an honest self-assessment to identify where you are on your journey, which areas need improvement, how balanced you are (i.e., mentally, physically, spiritually, and with those around you). It is essential to gauge your progress based on the last 30 days. Remember to be as truthful as possible (we're all grown here!)

Your accountability is key to your personal growth. You are not on this journey alone; keep in mind the people in your life that may have noticed a change, a change in habits, a change in your attitude, etc..

I find it useful to review the noticeable changes based on your logging and clutter pages within the last 30 days. It is so much you have repaired in your life. Take some time to reflect on how far you have come. Breathe in all of that beautiful growth and spiritual expansion! If you missed a few days and picked up where you left off, that is fine. It is all a process. It is still considered progress.

You have made it this far, and that is what matters most. You are willing to do the work. By doing the work, you should feel accomplished if not anything else. You continued to show up for yourself. On the following page are a few example questions to consider which may assist you with your self-review.

30 Day Review

Questions to consider...

- Is there more clutter as time progresses, or has your clarity and observations elevated?
- Do you have better control of your thoughts and actions? Have the affirmations helped on your journey?
- What needs your attention?
- Do you feel that your intuitive impulses are stronger?
- Are you reacting or retracting from things that may have been negative triggers in the past? How do you feel? Has your circle changed?
- Have the types of conversations you indulge in changed? Are you seeing yourself & others in a higher light? Do you feel more aligned?
- Have you released anxiety and worry with little to no effort over time?
- Did being attentive to your breath help you along your journey?
- How often did you need to increase meditation? Has your choice of clothing, food, travel changed?
- How often did you need to recenter daily?
- Do you feel as though you are in tune with your star player? Is your connection to your guides more fluid?
- Are you taking time to breathe and bring your being back to the present moment more easily?
- Are you more open and aware?
- Deja Vu?
- Past life memories, and how do they apply in your life at this time?

30 Day Review

When using any of the previous questions following up with the 'why or why not' is very important, these are just a few questions to help you assess your progress for the 30 days recently completed.

Moving Forward!

30 Day Review

30 Day Review

Next...

Now that you have reviewed your progress, you should be more comfortable and at ease with this journal and what you have accomplished in such a short time-frame; please keep the following in mind.

Sovereign Ruler of Self Check List:

- Self Awareness - clear perception of your own motives, character, thoughts, emotions, etc.
- Self Discipline - control of thoughts, actions/reactions, breath, etc.
- Self Transformation - the act, process, or result of transforming oneself
- Self Mastery - your body is your servant not your master; an active approach to life that may keep you in alignment with your star player

If you genuinely want to become more mindful, present, and aware, it is essential to know what you want to change, what you can change, and how you feel you can change these things. Making a conscious effort to change habits, patterns of behavior, and so forth is vital to your soul's growth in this lifetime. It is important to meditate, affirm, and speak life, not death, so that the subconscious mind can conspire with the universe to assist you along your journey. This journal is here to help you with self valuation and introspection.

NEXT 30 DAY IMPROVEMENT PLAN

10 THINGS YOU PLAN TO IMPROVE IN THE NEXT 30 DAYS:

May you accomplish all that you set out to in the next 30 days.

30 DAY IMPROVEMENT PLAN

Moving forward to your next 30 days!

Clear the Clutter

DATE: _____

A 90-DAY JOURNEY TO MINDFULNESS

Meditation:

AM Minutes _____

PM Minutes _____

Today's Affirmation:

AM Grattitude:

PM Gratttude:

Mindful Observations Today:

Mood Change: _____

Conscious Recenter/Refocus : _____

Subconscious Re-center/Refocus : _____

Clarity :

Clear the Clutter

DATE: _____

DATE: _____

AM MOOD ☺ ☹ 😣

PM MOOD ☺ ☹ 😣

Meditation:

AM Minutes _____

PM Minutes _____

Today's Affirmation:

AM Grattitude:

PM Gratttude:

Mindful Observations Today:

Mood Change: _____

Conscious Recenter/Refocus : _____

Subconscious Re-center/Refocus : _____

Clarity :

Clear the Clutter

DATE: _____

DATE: _____

AM MOOD ☺ ☹ 😩

PM MOOD ☺ ☹ 😩

Meditation:

AM Minutes _____

PM Minutes _____

Today's Affirmation:

AM Grattitude:

PM Gratttude:

Mindful Observations Today:

Mood Change: _____

Conscious Recenter/Refocus : _____

Subconscious Re-center/Refocus : _____

Clarity :

Clear the Clutter

DATE: _____

A 90-DAY JOURNEY TO MINDFULNESS

DATE: _____

AM MOOD   ☺ ☹ 😫

PM MOOD   ☺ ☹ 😫

Meditation:

AM Minutes _____

PM Minutes _____

Today's Affirmation:

AM Grattitude:

PM Gratttude:

Mindful Observations Today:

Mood Change: _____

Conscious Recenter/Refocus : _____

Subconscious Re-center/Refocus : _____

Clarity :

Clear the Clutter

DATE: _____

A 90-DAY JOURNEY TO MINDFULNESS

DATE: _____

AM MOOD

PM MOOD

Meditation:

AM Minutes _____

PM Minutes _____

Today's Affirmation:

AM Grattitude:

PM Gratttude:

Mindful Observations Today:

Mood Change: _____

Conscious Recenter/Refocus : _____

Subconscious Re-center/Refocus : _____

Clarity :

Clear the Clutter

DATE: _____

A 90-DAY JOURNEY TO
MINDFULNESS

DATE: _____

AM MOOD ☺ ☹ 😫

PM MOOD ☺ ☹ 😫

Meditation:

AM Minutes _____

PM Minutes _____

Today's Affirmation:

AM Grattitude:

PM Gratttude:

Mindful Observations Today:

Mood Change: _____

Conscious Recenter/Refocus : _____

Subconscious Re-center/Refocus : _____

Clarity :

Clear the Clutter

DATE: _____

A 90-DAY JOURNEY TO
MINDFULNESS

DATE: _____

AM MOOD ☺ ☹ 😫

PM MOOD ☺ ☹ 😫

Meditation:

AM Minutes _____

PM Minutes _____

Today's Affirmation:

AM Grattitude:

PM Gratttude:

Mindful Observations Today:

Mood Change: _____

Conscious Recenter/Refocus : _____

Subconscious Re-center/Refocus : _____

Clarity :

Clear the Clutter

DATE: _____

A 90-DAY JOURNEY TO
MINDFULNESS

DATE: _____

AM MOOD

PM MOOD ☺ ☹ 😫

Meditation:

AM Minutes _____

PM Minutes _____

Today's Affirmation:

AM Grattitude:

PM Gratttude:

Mindful Observations Today:

Mood Change: _____

Conscious Recenter/Refocus : _____

Subconscious Re-center/Refocus : _____

Clarity :

Clear the Clutter

DATE: _____

DATE: _____

AM MOOD

PM MOOD

Meditation:

AM Minutes _____

PM Minutes _____

Today's Affirmation:

AM Grattitude:

PM Gratttude:

Mindful Observations Today:

Mood Change: _____

Conscious Recenter/Refocus : _____

Subconscious Re-center/Refocus : _____

Clarity :

Clear the Clutter

DATE: _____

A 90-DAY JOURNEY TO MINDFULNESS

DATE: _____

AM MOOD

PM MOOD ☺ ☹ 😩

Meditation:

AM Minutes _____

PM Minutes _____

Today's Affirmation:

AM Grattitude:

PM Gratttude:

Mindful Observations Today:

Mood Change: _____

Conscious Recenter/Refocus : _____

Subconscious Re-center/Refocus : _____

Clarity :

Clear the Clutter

DATE: _____

A 90-DAY JOURNEY TO MINDFULNESS

DATE: _____

AM MOOD   ☺   ☹

PM MOOD   ☺   ☹   😫

Meditation:

AM Minutes _____

PM Minutes _____

Today's Affirmation:

AM Grattitude:

PM Gratttude:

Mindful Observations Today:

Mood Change: _____

Conscious Recenter/Refocus : _____

Subconscious Re-center/Refocus : _____

Clarity :

Clear the Clutter

DATE: _____

DATE: _____

AM MOOD ☺ ☹ 😣

PM MOOD ☺ ☹ 😣

Meditation:

AM Minutes _____

PM Minutes _____

Today's Affirmation:

AM Grattitude:

PM Gratttude:

Mindful Observations Today:

Mood Change: _____

Conscious Recenter/Refocus : _____

Subconscious Re-center/Refocus : _____

Clarity :

Clear the Clutter

DATE: _____

DATE: _____

AM MOOD

PM MOOD

Meditation:

AM Minutes _____

PM Minutes _____

Today's Affirmation:

AM Grattitude:

PM Gratttude:

Mindful Observations Today:

Mood Change: _____

Conscious Recenter/Refocus : _____

Subconscious Re-center/Refocus : _____

Clarity :

Clear the Clutter

DATE: _____

A 90-DAY JOURNEY TO MINDFULNESS

Meditation:

AM Minutes _____

PM Minutes _____

Today's Affirmation:

AM Grattitude:

PM Gratttude:

Mindful Observations Today:

Mood Change: _____

Conscious Recenter/Refocus : _____

Subconscious Re-center/Refocus : _____

Clarity :

Clear the Clutter

DATE: _____

A 90-DAY JOURNEY TO MINDFULNESS

DATE: _____

AM MOOD

PM MOOD ☺ ☹ 😫

Meditation:

AM Minutes _____

PM Minutes _____

Today's Affirmation:

AM Grattitude:

PM Gratttude:

Mindful Observations Today:

Mood Change: _____

Conscious Recenter/Refocus : _____

Subconscious Re-center/Refocus : _____

Clarity :

Clear the Clutter

DATE: _____

A 90-DAY JOURNEY TO MINDFULNESS

DATE: _____

AM MOOD

PM MOOD ☺ ☹ 😫

Meditation:

AM Minutes _____

PM Minutes _____

Today's Affirmation:

AM Grattitude:

PM Gratttude:

Mindful Observations Today:

Mood Change: _____

Conscious Recenter/Refocus : _____

Subconscious Re-center/Refocus : _____

Clarity :

Clear the Clutter

DATE: _____

Meditation:

AM Minutes _____

PM Minutes _____

Today's Affirmation:

AM Grattitude:

PM Gratttude:

Mindful Observations Today:

Mood Change: _____

Conscious Recenter/Refocus : _____

Subconscious Re-center/Refocus : _____

Clarity :

Clear the Clutter

DATE: _____

A 90-DAY JOURNEY TO MINDFULNESS

DATE: _____

AM MOOD

PM MOOD

Meditation:

AM Minutes _____

PM Minutes _____

Today's Affirmation:

AM Grattitude:

PM Gratttude:

Mindful Observations Today:

Mood Change: _____

Conscious Recenter/Refocus : _____

Subconscious Re-center/Refocus : _____

Clarity :

Clear the Clutter

DATE: _____

Meditation:

AM Minutes _____

PM Minutes _____

Today's Affirmation:

AM Grattitude:

PM Gratttude:

Mindful Observations Today:

Mood Change: _____

Conscious Recenter/Refocus : _____

Subconscious Re-center/Refocus :

Clarity :

Clear the Clutter

DATE: _____

A 90-DAY JOURNEY TO MINDFULNESS

DATE: _____

AM MOOD ☺ ☹ 😩

PM MOOD ☺ ☹ 😩

Meditation:

AM Minutes _____

PM Minutes _____

Today's Affirmation:

AM Grattitude:

PM Gratttude:

Mindful Observations Today:

Mood Change: _____

Conscious Recenter/Refocus : _____

Subconscious Re-center/Refocus : _____

Clarity :

Clear the Clutter

DATE: _____

DATE: _____

AM MOOD   ☺ ☹ 😫
PM MOOD   ☺ ☹ 😫

Meditation:

AM Minutes _____

PM Minutes _____

Today's Affirmation:

AM Grattitude:

PM Gratttude:

Mindful Observations Today:

Mood Change: _____

Conscious Recenter/Refocus : _____

Subconscious Re-center/Refocus : _____

Clarity :

Clear the Clutter

DATE: _____

A 90-DAY JOURNEY TO
MINDFULNESS

DATE: _____

AM MOOD

PM MOOD

Meditation:

AM Minutes _____

PM Minutes _____

Today's Affirmation:

AM Grattitude:

PM Gratttude:

Mindful Observations Today:

Mood Change: _____

Conscious Recenter/Refocus : _____

Subconscious Re-center/Refocus : _____

Clarity :

Clear the Clutter

DATE: _____

A 90-DAY JOURNEY TO MINDFULNESS

DATE: _____

AM MOOD   ☹ ☺

PM MOOD ☺ ☹ ☺

Meditation:

AM Minutes _____

PM Minutes _____

Today's Affirmation:

AM Grattitude:

PM Gratttude:

Mindful Observations Today:

Mood Change: _____

Conscious Recenter/Refocus : _____

Subconscious Re-center/Refocus : _____

Clarity :

Clear the Clutter

DATE: _____

A 90-DAY JOURNEY TO MINDFULNESS

DATE: _____

AM MOOD ☺ ☹ 😩

PM MOOD ☺ ☹ 😩

Meditation:

AM Minutes _____

PM Minutes _____

Today's Affirmation:

AM Grattitude:

PM Gratttude:

Mindful Observations Today:

Mood Change: _____

Conscious Recenter/Refocus : _____

Subconscious Re-center/Refocus : _____

Clarity :

Clear the Clutter

DATE: _____

A 90-DAY JOURNEY TO MINDFULNESS

DATE: _____

AM MOOD

PM MOOD

Meditation:

AM Minutes _____

PM Minutes _____

Today's Affirmation:

AM Grattitude:

PM Gratttude:

Mindful Observations Today:

Mood Change: _____

Conscious Recenter/Refocus : _____

Subconscious Re-center/Refocus : _____

Clarity :

Clear the Clutter

DATE: _____

DATE: _____

AM MOOD ☺ ☹ 😫

PM MOOD ☺ ☹ 😫

Meditation:

AM Minutes _____

PM Minutes _____

Today's Affirmation:

AM Grattitude:

PM Gratttude:

Mindful Observations Today:

Mood Change: _____

Conscious Recenter/Refocus : _____

Subconscious Re-center/Refocus : _____

Clarity :

Clear the Clutter

DATE: _____

Meditation:

AM Minutes _____

PM Minutes _____

Today's Affirmation:

AM Grattitude:

PM Gratttude:

Mindful Observations Today:

Mood Change: _____

Conscious Recenter/Refocus : _____

Subconscious Re-center/Refocus : _____

Clarity :

Clear the Clutter

DATE: _____

A 90-DAY JOURNEY TO
MINDFULNESS

DATE: _____

AM MOOD ☺ ☹ 😫
PM MOOD ☺ ☹ 😫

Meditation:

AM Minutes _____

PM Minutes _____

Today's Affirmation:

AM Grattitude:

PM Gratttude:

Mindful Observations Today:

Mood Change: _____

Conscious Recenter/Refocus : _____

Subconscious Re-center/Refocus : _____

Clarity :

Clear the Clutter

DATE: _____

A 90-DAY JOURNEY TO MINDFULNESS

Meditation:

AM Minutes _____

PM Minutes _____

Today's Affirmation:

AM Grattitude:

PM Gratttude:

Mindful Observations Today:

Mood Change: _____

Conscious Recenter/Refocus : _____

Subconscious Re-center/Refocus : _____

Clarity :

Clear the Clutter

DATE: _____

A 90-DAY JOURNEY TO MINDFULNESS

DATE: _____

AM MOOD   ☺ ☹ 😖

PM MOOD   ☺ ☹ 😖

Meditation:

AM Minutes _____

PM Minutes _____

Today's Affirmation:

AM Grattitude:

PM Gratttude:

Mindful Observations Today:

Mood Change: _____

Conscious Recenter/Refocus : _____

Subconscious Re-center/Refocus : _____

Clarity :

60 Day Review

Repition forms habit. Let's do this again.

Now you have reached another milestone. Booyah! Here lies yet another honest self-assessment to identify where you are on your journey, which areas need improvement, how balanced you are (i.e., mentally, physically, spiritually, and those around you). It is crucial to gauge your progress based on the last 30 days. Remember to be as truthful as possible (we're all grown here!)

Your accountability is key to your personal growth. You are not on this journey alone; keep in mind the people in your life that may have noticed a change, a change in habits, a change in your attitude, etc..

I find it useful to review the noticeable changes based on your logging and clutter pages within the last 30 days. It is so much you have repaired in your life. Take some time to reflect on how far you have come. Breathe in all of that beautiful growth and spiritual expansion! If you missed a few days and picked up where you left off, that is fine. It is all a process. It is still considered progress.

You have made it this far, and that is what matters most. You are willing to do the work. By doing the work, you should feel accomplished, if not anything else. You continued to show up for yourself. On the following page are a few example questions to consider which may assist you with your self-review.

60 Day Review

Questions to consider...

- Is there more clutter as time progresses, or has your clarity and observations elevated?
- Do you have better control of your thoughts and actions? Have the affirmations helped on your journey?
- What needs your attention?
- Do you feel that your intuitive impulses are more vital?
- Are you reacting or retracting from things that may have been negative triggers in the past?
- How do you feel? Has your circle changed?
- Have the types of conversations you indulge in changed?
- Are you seeing yourself & others in a higher light?
- Do you feel more aligned?
- Have you released anxiety and worry with little to no effort over time?
- Did being attentive to your breath help you along your journey?
- How often did you need to increase meditation? Has your choice of clothing, food, travel changed?
- How often did you need to recenter daily?
- Do you feel as though you are in tune with your star player?
- Is your connection to your guides more fluid?
- Are you taking time to breathe and bring your being back to the present moment more easily?
- Are you more open and aware?
- Deja Vu?
- Past life memories, and how do they apply in your life at this time?

60 Day Review

Using any of the previous questions following up with the 'why or why not' is very important; these are just a few questions to help you assess your progress for the 30 days recently completed.

Moving Forward!

60 Day Review

60 Day Review

Next...

After reviewing your progress, you should know what you have accomplished in such a short time-frame; please keep the following in mind.

Sovereign Ruler of Self Check List:

- Self Awareness - clear perception of your own motives, character, thoughts, emotions, etc.
- Self Discipline - control of thoughts, actions/reactions, breath, etc.
- Self Transformation - the act, process, or result of transforming oneself
- Self Mastery - your body is your servant not your master; an active approach to life that may keep you in alignment with your star player

If you genuinely want to become more mindful and aware, it is essential to know what you want to change, what you can change, and how you feel you can change these things. Making a conscious effort to change habits, patterns of behavior, etc. is vital to your soul's growth in this lifetime. It is important to meditate, affirm, and speak life, not death, so that the subconscious mind can conspire with the universe to assist you along your journey. This journal is here to help you with self valuation and introspection.

NEXT 30 DAY
IMPROVEMENT PLAN

10 THINGS YOU PLAN TO IMPROVE IN THE NEXT 30 DAYS:

May you accomplish all that you set out to in the next 30 days.

Moving forward!

Clear the Clutter

DATE: _____

DATE: _____

AM MOOD

PM MOOD

Meditation:

AM Minutes _____

PM Minutes _____

Today's Affirmation:

AM Grattitude:

PM Gratttude:

Mindful Observations Today:

Mood Change: _____

Conscious Recenter/Refocus : _____

Subconscious Re-center/Refocus : _____

Clarity :

Clear the Clutter

DATE: _____

A 90-DAY JOURNEY TO
MINDFULNESS

DATE: _____

AM MOOD

PM MOOD ☺ ☹ 😫

Meditation:

AM Minutes _____

PM Minutes _____

Today's Affirmation:

AM Grattitude:

PM Gratttude:

Mindful Observations Today:

Mood Change: _____

Conscious Recenter/Refocus : _____

Subconscious Re-center/Refocus :

Clarity :

Clear the Clutter

DATE: _____

A 90-DAY JOURNEY TO MINDFULNESS

AM MOOD ☺ ☹ 😫

PM MOOD ☺ ☹ 😫

Meditation:

AM Minutes ____

PM Minutes ____

Today's Affirmation:

AM Grattitude:

PM Gratttude:

Mindful Observations Today:

Mood Change: ____

Conscious Recenter/Refocus : ____

Subconscious Re-center/Refocus :

Clarity :

Clear the Clutter

DATE: _____

A 90-DAY JOURNEY TO MINDFULNESS

DATE: _____

AM MOOD   ☺ ☹ 😫

PM MOOD   ☺ ☹ 😫

Meditation:

AM Minutes _____

PM Minutes _____

Today's Affirmation:

AM Grattitude:

PM Gratttude:

Mindful Observations Today:

Mood Change: _____

Conscious Recenter/Refocus : _____

Subconscious Re-center/Refocus : _____

Clarity :

Clear the Clutter

DATE: _____

A 90-DAY JOURNEY TO MINDFULNESS

DATE: _____

AM MOOD ☺ ☹ 😖

PM MOOD ☺ ☹ 😖

Meditation:

AM Minutes _____

PM Minutes _____

Today's Affirmation:

AM Grattitude:

PM Gratttude:

Mindful Observations Today:

Mood Change: _____

Conscious Recenter/Refocus : _____

Subconscious Re-center/Refocus : _____

Clarity :

Clear the Clutter

DATE: _____

A 90-DAY JOURNEY TO
MINDFULNESS

DATE: _____

AM MOOD ☺ ☹ 😫

PM MOOD ☺ ☹ 😫

Meditation:

AM Minutes _____

PM Minutes _____

Today's Affirmation:

AM Grattitude:

PM Gratttude:

Mindful Observations Today:

Mood Change: _____

Conscious Recenter/Refocus : _____

Subconscious Re-center/Refocus : _____

Clarity :

Clear the Clutter

DATE: _____

A 90-DAY JOURNEY TO MINDFULNESS

DATE: _____

AM MOOD ☺ ☹ 😫

PM MOOD ☺ ☹ 😫

Meditation:

AM Minutes _____

PM Minutes _____

Today's Affirmation:

AM Grattitude:

PM Gratttude:

Mindful Observations Today:

Mood Change: _____

Conscious Recenter/Refocus : _____

Subconscious Re-center/Refocus : _____

Clarity :

Clear the Clutter

DATE: _____

DATE: _____

AM MOOD ☺ ☹ �©

PM MOOD ☺ ☹ 😩

Meditation:

AM Minutes _____

PM Minutes _____

Today's Affirmation:

AM Grattitude:

PM Gratttude:

Mindful Observations Today:

Mood Change: _____

Conscious Recenter/Refocus : _____

Subconscious Re-center/Refocus : _____

Clarity :

Clear the Clutter

DATE: _____

DATE: _____

AM MOOD ☺ ☹ 😫

PM MOOD ☺ ☹ 😫

Meditation:

AM Minutes _____

PM Minutes _____

Today's Affirmation:

AM Grattitude:

PM Gratttude:

Mindful Observations Today:

Mood Change: _____

Conscious Recenter/Refocus : _____

Subconscious Re-center/Refocus :
_____

Clarity :

Clear the Clutter

DATE: _____

A 90-DAY JOURNEY TO MINDFULNESS

DATE: _____

AM MOOD ☺ ☹ 😫

PM MOOD ☺ ☹ 😫

Meditation:

AM Minutes _____

PM Minutes _____

Today's Affirmation:

AM Grattitude:

PM Gratttude:

Mindful Observations Today:

Mood Change: _____

Conscious Recenter/Refocus : _____

Subconscious Re-center/Refocus : _____

Clarity :

Clear the Clutter

DATE: _____

A 90-DAY JOURNEY TO MINDFULNESS

DATE: _____

AM MOOD

PM MOOD

Meditation:

AM Minutes _____

PM Minutes _____

Today's Affirmation:

AM Grattitude:

PM Gratttude:

Mindful Observations Today:

Mood Change: _____

Conscious Recenter/Refocus : _____

Subconscious Re-center/Refocus : _____

Clarity :

Clear the Clutter

DATE: _____

A 90-DAY JOURNEY TO
MINDFULNESS

Meditation:

AM Minutes _____

PM Minutes _____

Today's Affirmation:

AM Grattitude:

PM Gratttude:

Mindful Observations Today:

Mood Change: _____

Conscious Recenter/Refocus : _____

Subconscious Re-center/Refocus : _____

Clarity :

Clear the Clutter

DATE: _____

A 90-DAY JOURNEY TO MINDFULNESS

DATE: _____

AM MOOD ☺ ☹ 😫

PM MOOD ☺ ☹ 😫

Meditation:

AM Minutes _____

PM Minutes _____

Today's Affirmation:

AM Grattitude:

PM Gratttude:

Mindful Observations Today:

Mood Change: _____

Conscious Recenter/Refocus : _____

Subconscious Re-center/Refocus : _____

Clarity : _____

Clear the Clutter

DATE: _____

A 90-DAY JOURNEY TO
MINDFULNESS

DATE: _____

AM MOOD

PM MOOD ☺ ☹ 😫

Meditation:

AM Minutes ____

PM Minutes ____

Today's Affirmation:

AM Grattitude:

PM Gratttude:

Mindful Observations Today:

Mood Change: _____

Conscious Recenter/Refocus : _____

Subconscious Re-center/Refocus :

_____

Clarity :

Clear the Clutter

DATE: _____

A 90-DAY JOURNEY TO MINDFULNESS

DATE: _____

AM MOOD

PM MOOD 😊 ☹ 😩

Meditation:

AM Minutes _____

PM Minutes _____

Today's Affirmation:

AM Grattitude:

PM Gratttude:

Mindful Observations Today:

Mood Change: _____

Conscious Recenter/Refocus : _____

Subconscious Re-center/Refocus :

Clarity :

Clear the Clutter

DATE: _____

A 90-DAY JOURNEY TO
MINDFULNESS

DATE: _____

AM MOOD

PM MOOD

Meditation:

AM Minutes _____

PM Minutes _____

Today's Affirmation:

AM Grattitude:

PM Gratttude:

Mindful Observations Today:

Mood Change: _____

Conscious Recenter/Refocus : _____

Subconscious Re-center/Refocus : _____

Clarity :

Clear the Clutter

DATE: _____

A 90-DAY JOURNEY TO MINDFULNESS

Meditation:

AM Minutes _____

PM Minutes _____

Today's Affirmation:

AM Grattitude:

PM Gratttude:

Mindful Observations Today:

Mood Change: _____

Conscious Recenter/Refocus : _____

Subconscious Re-center/Refocus : _____

Clarity :

Clear the Clutter

DATE: _____

A 90-DAY JOURNEY TO
MINDFULNESS

A 90-DAY JOURNEY TO
MINDFULNESS

DATE: _____

AM MOOD   ☺ ☹ 😫

PM MOOD   ☺ ☹ 😫

Meditation:

AM Minutes _____

PM Minutes _____

Today's Affirmation:

AM Grattitude:

PM Gratttude:

Mindful Observations Today:

Mood Change: _____

Conscious Recenter/Refocus : _____

Subconscious Re-center/Refocus :

Clarity :

Clear the Clutter

DATE: _____

A 90-DAY JOURNEY TO MINDFULNESS

Meditation:

AM Minutes _____

PM Minutes _____

Today's Affirmation:

AM Grattitude:

PM Gratttude:

Mindful Observations Today:

Mood Change: _____

Conscious Recenter/Refocus : _____

Subconscious Re-center/Refocus : _____

Clarity :

Clear the Clutter

DATE: _____

A 90-DAY JOURNEY TO MINDFULNESS

DATE: _____

AM MOOD   ☺ ☹ 😫

PM MOOD   ☺ ☹ 😫

Meditation:

AM Minutes _____

PM Minutes _____

Today's Affirmation:

AM Grattitude:

PM Gratttude:

Mindful Observations Today:

Mood Change: _____

Conscious Recenter/Refocus : _____

Subconscious Re-center/Refocus : _____

Clarity :

Clear the Clutter

DATE: _____

A 90-DAY JOURNEY TO MINDFULNESS

DATE: _____

AM MOOD

PM MOOD ☺ ☹ 😫

Meditation:

AM Minutes _____

PM Minutes _____

Today's Affirmation:

AM Grattitude:

PM Gratttude:

Mindful Observations Today:

Mood Change: _____

Conscious Recenter/Refocus : _____

Subconscious Re-center/Refocus : _____

Clarity :

Clear the Clutter

DATE: _____

A 90-DAY JOURNEY TO
MINDFULNESS

DATE: _____

AM MOOD ☺ ☹ 😫

PM MOOD ☺ ☹ 😫

Meditation:

AM Minutes _____

PM Minutes _____

Today's Affirmation:

AM Grattitude:

PM Gratttude:

Mindful Observations Today:

Mood Change: _____

Conscious Recenter/Refocus : _____

Subconscious Re-center/Refocus : _____

Clarity :

Clear the Clutter

DATE: _____

A 90-DAY JOURNEY TO MINDFULNESS

DATE: _____

AM MOOD

PM MOOD

Meditation:

AM Minutes _____

PM Minutes _____

Today's Affirmation:

AM Grattitude:

PM Gratttude:

Mindful Observations Today:

Mood Change: _____

Conscious Recenter/Refocus : _____

Subconscious Re-center/Refocus :
_____

Clarity :

Clear the Clutter

DATE: _____

A 90-DAY JOURNEY TO MINDFULNESS

DATE: _____

AM MOOD

PM MOOD

Meditation:

AM Minutes _____

PM Minutes _____

Today's Affirmation:

AM Grattitude:

PM Gratttude:

Mindful Observations Today:

Mood Change: _____

Conscious Recenter/Refocus : _____

Subconscious Re-center/Refocus : _____

Clarity :

Clear the Clutter

DATE: _____

DATE: _____

AM MOOD

PM MOOD

Meditation:

AM Minutes _____

PM Minutes _____

Today's Affirmation:

AM Grattitude:

PM Gratttude:

Mindful Observations Today:

Mood Change: _____

Conscious Recenter/Refocus : _____

Subconscious Re-center/Refocus : _____

Clarity :

Clear the Clutter

DATE: _____

A 90-DAY JOURNEY TO MINDFULNESS

DATE: _____

AM MOOD

PM MOOD   ☺ ☹ 😫

Meditation:

AM Minutes _____

PM Minutes _____

Today's Affirmation:

AM Grattitude:

PM Gratttude:

Mindful Observations Today:

Mood Change: _____

Conscious Recenter/Refocus : _____

Subconscious Re-center/Refocus :
_____

Clarity :

Clear the Clutter

DATE: _____

A 90-DAY JOURNEY TO MINDFULNESS

DATE: _____

AM MOOD ☺ ☹ 😫

PM MOOD ☺ ☹ 😫

Meditation:

AM Minutes _____

PM Minutes _____

Today's Affirmation:

AM Grattitude:

PM Gratttude:

Mindful Observations Today:

Mood Change: _____

Conscious Recenter/Refocus : _____

Subconscious Re-center/Refocus : _____

Clarity :

Clear the Clutter

DATE: _____

A 90-DAY JOURNEY TO
MINDFULNESS

DATE: _____

AM MOOD ☺ ☹ 😫

PM MOOD ☺ ☹ 😫

Meditation:

AM Minutes _____

PM Minutes _____

Today's Affirmation:

AM Grattitude:

PM Gratttude:

Mindful Observations Today:

Mood Change: _____

Conscious Recenter/Refocus : _____

Subconscious Re-center/Refocus : _____

Clarity :

Clear the Clutter

DATE: _____

DATE: _____

AM MOOD

PM MOOD ☺ ☹ 😖

Meditation:

AM Minutes _____

PM Minutes _____

Today's Affirmation:

AM Grattitude:

PM Gratttude:

Mindful Observations Today:

Mood Change: _____

Conscious Recenter/Refocus : _____

Subconscious Re-center/Refocus : _____

Clarity :

Clear the Clutter

DATE: _____

A 90-DAY JOURNEY TO MINDFULNESS

Meditation:

AM Minutes _____

PM Minutes _____

Today's Affirmation:

AM Grattitude:

PM Gratttude:

Mindful Observations Today:

Mood Change: _____

Conscious Recenter/Refocus : _____

Subconscious Re-center/Refocus : _____

Clarity :

90 Day Review

Let's Review your growth!

Now you have reached your 90-day check-up. As mentioned in your previous 30-day reviews; This should also be another honest self-assessment to identify where you are on your journey, which areas need improvement, how balanced you are at this time on your journey (i.e., mentally, physically, spiritually, and with those around you). It is crucial to gauge your progress based on the last 60 days. Remember to be as truthful as possible (we're all grown here!)

Your accountability is key to your personal growth. You are not on this journey alone; keep in mind the people in your life that may have noticed a change, a change in habits, a change in your attitude, etc.. Everything you touch, you change, and everything you change in turn changes you.

I find it effective to review the noticeable changes based on your logging and clutter pages within the last 60 days. It is so much you have repaired in your life. Take some time to reflect on how far you have come. Breathe in all of that beautiful growth and spiritual expansion!

You have made it! 90-days of effort, time, and energy focused on personal and physical growth. You have done the work. By doing the work, you should feel accomplished, if not anything else. You continued to show up for yourself and should proceed to do so.

90 Day Review & Evolution

It's time to sum it all up!

Here is your final assessment of the journey you decided to embark upon. You may use the 30-day review pages, self-observations, the A.S.E. Worksheets, and the following sample questions to re-examine your journey.

I have included the following items you may use as a guidepost to reflect and review your accomplishments.

Using the lined pages that follow, you may freely express and be amazed by who you have become in as little as three months.

The following page, titled 90 Day Evolution Review, can be used as a tool to name and claim your current state of being or how you view yourself in the next 90 days.

90 Day Review

Did you meet or exceed your initial expectations (p.1, s1)?

Has your anxiety, adhd, depression, etc. become manageable?

Are you receiving and acting on your intuitive nudges without second thought?

Do you feel accomplished overall?

Is your ability to recognize psychic attacks easier to identify?

Has your re-alignment process become automatic at least 90% of the time?

Have you been able to sit in the midst of storms with calm clarity?

Do you feel more aligned with your higher self?

By raising your vibration and frequency have you attracted more of your tribe?

Have you made spending time alone a priority?

Has changing your self talk improved?

90 Day Review

Are you even more of a believer in the POSSIBLE?

Are mindful practices and interactions a way of life now?

Is your connection to your guides more fluid when receiving and accepting information?

Has your meditation practices enhanced to a new level?

Can you pretty much pinpoint the meaning of your dreams without research?

Is your creativity at it's highest peak and the way in which you express yourself?

Are you more aware of your breathing (i.e. shallow breathing vs. full breaths)?

Have you noticed the illusion of time, can you bend time now?

Has your sense of urgency decreased?

Is your ability to multitask far more easier than in months past?

Has your use of social media, tel-lie-vision, etc decreased significantly?

Do you focus more on things you can control rather than those you can

90 Day Review

Do you find yourself wanting to go outside more?

Has your diet improved?

Have you stopped taking yourself too seriously?

Do you sometimes allow your mind to wonder about (inner child work)?

Is your ability to multitask far more easier than in months past?

Has your use of social media, tel-lie-vision, etc decreased significantly?

Is there a need to seek new experiences, travel, or education/new line of study?

Are you smiling more?

Have your communication improved?

Did you feel the need to minimize your circle of friends, possessions, or overall
lifestyle?

90 Day Review

90 Day Review

90 Day Review

90 DAY EVOLUTION

:

90 DAY EVOLUTION

:

90 DAY EVOLUTION

:

THE JOURNEY CONTINUES

Congratulations! You are just getting started..
Enjoy your journey, friend.

Notes

DATE: _____

Notes

DATE: _____

Notes

DATE: _____

Notes

DATE: _____

Notes

DATE: _____

Notes

DATE: _____

Notes

DATE: _____

Notes

DATE: _____

Notes

DATE: _____

Notes

DATE: _____

Notes

DATE: _____

Notes

DATE: _____

Notes

DATE: _____

Notes

DATE: _____

Notes

DATE: _____

Notes

DATE: _____

Notes

DATE: _____

Notes

DATE: _____

Notes

DATE: _____

Notes

DATE: _____

Notes

DATE: _____

Notes

DATE: _____

Notes

DATE: _____

Notes

DATE: _____

Notes

DATE: _____

Notes

DATE: _____

Notes

DATE: _____

Notes

DATE: _____

Notes

DATE: _____